Public Access Information

The owner allows extensive public access to the forest even though it is private property. With the exception of one footpath, called Church Walk, there are no public rights of way.

To prevent the creation of vehicular rights of way, the forest's roads are closed on one day annually. This is usually on the first working day of the year.

Apart from that day, the owner allows cars to be driven along the Grand Avenue and a few other main avenues not blocked by a barrier as long as the speed limit of 20mph is observed.

On foot, most parts of the forest are accessible. However, there are a number of private dwellings and visitors are asked to respect the privacy of the residents.

The Forestry Commission carries out work including the felling of trees so do take notice of any warning signs that you may come across.

Signage is kept to a minimum; do not expect any signposts or road names.

Use the map to find ··· round and ·· t and es, a aths ybe ain ...e wet

Camping is restricted to the campsite at Postern Hill. Near the campsite is a beautiful picnic and barbecue area, but all other camping and lighting of fires is strictly forbidden.

The safest place to park your car is at the Postern Hill site, but you may park anywhere that doesn't interfere with forestry work or other car drivers. But please do not leave any valuables in your vehicle.

Dog owners are asked to keep their dogs under control, and that poo is kept off the paths by moving it into the undergrowth where it can decompose naturally.

Any organised activity within the forest must have permission in advance from the Savernake Estate and the Forestry Commission.

Main Gate

INTRODUCTION

Savernake is Britain's only privately owned forest and it has been in the care of the same family for nearly a thousand years.

The name first appears in the Domesday Book as Safernoc which is thought to mean fern and oak, although some think it may have derived from the word 'savhr' meaning gravel. This description may be appropriate as there is a layer of flint over the underlying chalk plateau.

Through the centre of the forest is the Grand Avenue which is the longest tree-lined avenue in Britain at four miles in length. An anonymous writer in the 1800s described it like this:

"There is a continuous Gothic arch of green for miles, beneath which one may walk as in the aisles of a forest abbey."

People often have similar responses to being in a cathedral

> The Grand Avenue is the longest avenue of trees in Britain.

and being in a forest. It can inspire feelings of euphoria, wonder and humility, and at the same time can be reassuringly comforting.

Savernake is a remnant of primeval forest that has never been cleared and as such provides a unique environment for wildlife. There are thriving colonies of some species that have become extinct in other parts of the country.

Although old, it was not left to its own devices. It has always been under a system of management, overseen by the Warden, working hand in hand with nature. Trees have been almost continually planted to replace ones felled. Wood was, of course, used much more widely

for burning as well as for building before other more modern methods were introduced.

Not only is Savernake a site of important ecological interest, it also has a rich and varied history. New technology has been able to 'look through' the trees from above and map out the contours of the forest floor. It has revealed evidence of Prehistoric and Iron Age settlements. The remains of two Roman roads run through the forest and a Roman tessellated pavement was discovered very close to Tottenham House, which is thought to have been the site of a villa.

One of the highlights of Savernake's history was during King Henry VIII's reign. His third wife, Jane Seymour, was born and raised in the forest at Wolfhall, and it was at this house that the King stayed on several occasions.

Another well-known name associated with the forest was

Milestone on A346

The Grand Avenue

Lancelot 'Capability' Brown who was responsible for designing the large number of drives and avenues including the Grand Avenue. The way the forest looks today is largely down to his foresight and extensive tree planting programme.

At one time, there were as many as five tree nurseries nurturing saplings through their first few years. They needed protecting from the large number of deer that would have easily finished them off. Sadly these days, there are no longer any working nurseries in the forest.

The forest only covers a fraction of the 100 square miles it did in the year 1200. After that time, woodlands became uneconomic and were, over a long period, drastically reduced in size. Today Savernake covers an area of just over 7 square miles.

The forest has been designated an Area of Outstanding Natural Beauty and is also a Site of Special Scientific Interest.

Forestry Commission at work

FORESTRY COMMISSION

In 1939, the Forestry Commission signed a 999-year lease with the Savernake Estate to take over the management of the trees.

The Forestry Commission is a non-ministerial government department established in 1919 and is responsible for sustainable woodland management throughout Britain. It also promotes the benefits of forests for nature conservation and for public recreation.

Their work includes timber harvesting, replanting felled areas, maintaining and improving the environment for wildlife, and providing easy access for the public.

Forest management is a long-term business and Britain's timber industry is growing. It is essential to have a system of harvesting and replanting which will continue the supply of wood into the future.

In Savernake, they have a detailed plan of action for periods of five years at a time, and that is part of a much broader fifty-year strategy.

Recent work has included surveying and tagging more than 7,000 veteran trees with the help of global positioning systems, and clearing the areas around them to give them more light and room to breathe.

In the early days of the Forestry Commission, they planted large expanses of conifer trees because they were quick to grow and would create a quick

The timber rights have been leased to the Forestry Commission for 999 years.

4

financial return. They were criticised for this, and so were prevented from doing the same in Savernake as one of the conditions of the lease.

However, there are still some areas of conifer. Birch Copse is now almost entirely a conifer plantation. They also planted a pine arboretum just off the Grand Avenue in the Braydon area.

The policy now is to never replant broadleaf trees such as oak and beech with softwoods, but softwoods are replanted if harvested. The broadleaf areas of the forest are allowed to naturally regenerate.

Due to the demand of people wanting to camp in the forest, the

Forestry Commission opened a campsite in the 1960s at Postern Hill. It is now run by Forest Holidays in partnership with the Forestry Commission and the Camping and Caravanning Club. Nearby, permanent barbecue hearths and picnic benches are also provided for visitors at this the highest point in the forest.

Barbecue site at Postern Hill

Monument near Grand Avenue

MONUMENTS & MEMORIALS

The Ailesbury Column stands 28 metres (90 feet) high and is the most recognised monument in the forest. It had once stood in Hammersmith for twenty years in memory of someone else until Thomas Bruce Brudenell, the Earl of Ailesbury, bought it for Savernake in 1781.

He placed two new inscriptions on it. The first gave thanks for the recovery of the King to good health. But when the King later had a relapse and died, he was persuaded by 'Capability' Brown to add another plaque on the opposite side. This one stated his gratitude to his uncle for leaving Savernake to him, and secondly his loyalty to the King.

A smaller, not so well known, monument is situated about two-thirds along the Grand Avenue from the main gate on the right-hand side. It is built of stone and is surrounded by iron railings. There is no inscription but it is thought to be a memorial to someone who died in a riding accident.

There is a ghost story, which may or may not be connected. A young lady was riding through the forest with a royal hunting party when her horse suddenly bolted through the trees. She was decapitated by a low branch and her headless ghost is sometimes seen riding on horseback.

In the eastern side of Savernake, past Crockmere Oak and pool, there is a small gravestone beside the road which can be overgrown and hard to find. It commemorates Gerald Saul Posner who died in 1994. He was a deer stalker in the forest and while he was carrying the carcass of a fully grown buck he collapsed of a heart attack and died.

Gravestone

Bluebells in May

FLORA AND FAUNA

Savernake today is a mixed broadleaved forest of mostly beech and oak with a few coniferous plantations although there are many other species present such as ash, rowan and hazel.

What you find in the forest will depend largely on the time of year. In spring, the forest begins to burst into life. Leaves are a bright, fresh green and in some areas bluebells carpet the ground.

In autumn, the forest changes dramatically into a golden wonderland. It can be magical being under beech trees watching the leaves gently fall into deep drifts that crunch satisfyingly underfoot.

The beeches tend to have shallow roots and large specimens can become top heavy and fall over. In the storms of 1990, Savernake lost 700 beeches and 50 oaks in the extreme winds.

The oak is a close relative of the beech but has a much longer lifespan. Where the beech can live to 250 years, the oak can live to more than four times that length.

The ancient oaks in Savernake were established trees at the turn of the first millennium and are now well over a thousand years old. When they were young, oak was the predominant tree in the forest. Even since Prehistoric times, it was the preferred tree because it

> **An oak
> sustains more life
> than any other tree.**

7

Beeches in late autumn

is strong and durable and also burns slowly with a steady flame. Its charcoal is a premium product which can be used for metal-working.

They can take up to fifty years to reach maturity and play a unique part of the forest's ecosystem. One mature oak can be home to up to 350 types of insects alone and these are eaten by a large number of other birds and animals which find shelter in the branches or hollow trunks.

Unlike the beech, their bark is ridged and rough allowing a variety of lichens, mosses, fungi and even ferns to get a hold.

The forest lies on a plateau of

More than 500 types of fungi can be found in the forest.

chalk covered by clay with flints and has four valleys running through it. The clay in the valley bottoms can often become muddy even though there are no streams or rivers running along them. Instead, there are numerous pools that provide water for wildlife,

Oak bark

and habitats for dragonflies and great-crested newts. The pools at twilight are a good place to see bats where they swoop with great accuracy to drink tiny drops of water at a time.

There are seventeen species of bats in Britain and of these; eleven have been identified in Savernake. The abundance of hollow trees and insects make it an ideal environment for them to live.

Shaggy Parasol

© Arco Images GmbH / Alamy

© imagebroker / Alamy

Bechstein Bat

The rare barbastelle and bechstein bats both have colonies in Savernake, but the most common variety is the pipistrelle which is about 4cm long and can eat as many as 3,000 insects in one night. All species of bat are protected under the Wildlife and Countryside Act. Anyone disturbing a bat or its roost can be punished with a heavy fine or even imprisonment.

The Bat Conservation Trust works with the Forestry Commission to ensure the bats have suitable conditions to thrive.

Much of the Savernake area has been designated as a Site of Special Scientific Interest. These are sites recognised for having some of the most important biodiversity in the country. Due to its unique conditions it provides habitats for wildlife, plants and fungi that are not present elsewhere.

As well as many lichens and mosses, Savernake has well over 500 species of fungi. This exceptional number can be put down to the fact that dead wood is not cleared but left to decay where it falls.

Red Kite

© John Cancalosi / Alamy

The forest is rich in wildlife. Twenty-five types of butterfly breed in the area including the white letter hairstreak and the elusive purple emperor.

Redstarts, nuthatches, turtle doves, nightingales and wood-peckers are only a few of the many bird populations that have made a home here. Not to mention the birds of prey such as owls, buzzards and sparrowhawks; even a pair of red kites has recently taken up residence. These large birds can be identified by their chestnut red bodies with white patches under their wings, a deeply forked tail and a wing span of about five feet.

There are, of course, many foxes, badgers, countless squirrels

Dormice are extinct in seven counties in England.

Dormouse is derived from 'dormeus' which means sleepy (one).

and dormice. These small mouse-like rodents are now extinct in seven counties in England and are fully protected.

As nocturnal animals, they spend most of their nights in the branches of trees looking for fruit, nuts and flowers to eat. They partic-ularly like hazel and are sometimes known as hazel dormice. A discarded hazelnut shell with a smooth-edged round hole in it is a sure sign of their presence.

If food is scarce or if it is partic-ularly cold and wet, they will curl themselves up in a ball and sleep to conserve energy until things improve. In fact, they spend most of their lives asleep because, in addition to their summer naps,

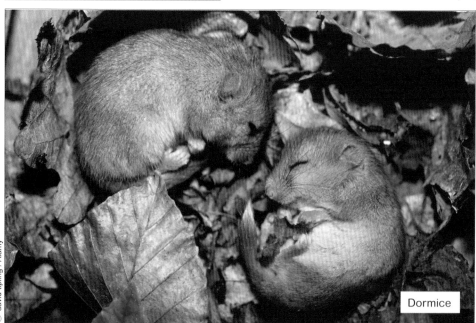

Dormice

Fallow Deer

© Arco Images GmbH / Alamy

they hibernate from October to late April.

They sometimes choose to make their nests in a hollow tree or in a bird box, but most often they will make them under the deep leaf litter on the forest floor where, unfortunately, they are in danger of being trampled by deer.

Fallow, roe and muntjac deer are all living wild in the forest and if you are lucky you may encounter these beautiful animals.

Although they are active throughout the day and night, they are most likely seen at either dawn or dusk. During the day, they tend to lie up to ruminate between feeding.

Unfortunately, they do a huge amount of damage to young trees especially young beeches and oaks

Antlers are shed each year at the end of the mating season.

Deer are most likely seen at dawn or dusk.

which seem to be particular favourites. Their numbers have to be managed by a trained deer stalker during the legal stalking season.

The red deer is our largest land mammal standing more than a metre at shoulder level. The stags have highly branched antlers that in Neolithic times were used as tools. Although there are no red deer in the forest, there are some living in the deer park near Tottenham House.

The fallow deer is slightly smaller and can be recognised by their tan coat with white spots. The males are the only British deer to have palmate antlers and because of their ornamental nature, they were a prized species on royal hunting trips.

Roe Deer

© blickwinkle / Alamy

The roe deer is our smallest native deer, although they had to be reintroduced into the country from Scotland after they became extinct in the eighteenth century. Their coats are a rich, foxy red in the summer and the males have short antlers with three tines on each. They are usually recognised by their white rump which you see as they run away.

Although they tend to be solitary animals, they will form small groups in winter. They have their kids in May or June and will often have twins or triplets. These newborns can sometimes be found unexpectedly in the undergrowth, but they have not been abandoned. Their mother will be somewhere nearby and will return to suckle them.

Roe deer often have twins or triplets.

The other species of deer you may come across is the muntjac. They were introduced to this country from China in the early part of the twentieth century and are now widespread in the wild. They are the smallest deer found in Savernake and although their numbers are increasing, they are not thought to be as destructive as other types of deer.

Roe Deer twins

© Chris Fredriksson / Alamy

POLLARDING

A lot of the older trees in Savernake have been pollarded. It is a type of tree pruning which enables a regular supply of wood to be taken without the need for chopping the tree down, and was popular when wood was in huge demand everyday.

The idea is similar to coppicing where a tree is cut to encourage the growth of multiple stems, but instead of cutting the trunk at ground level, the tree is cut at just over head height. Pollarding is preferred when deer are around because they cannot reach to eat the new emerging shoots.

The resulting branches require regular maintenance with pruning carried out every two to five years.

A characteristic of old pollards is a hollow trunk which makes them difficult to age accurately.

However, the process has been found to extend the life of the tree but only if done from a young age.

Beeches and oaks both do well under this kind of management. But about 150 years ago, the craft died out in Savernake and the neglected trees were left to grow and develop enormous branches resulting in some truly amazing shapes. Unfortunately, the weight of some of the branches has become too much for the hollow trunks to support and have broken off splitting the trunk in the process.

Pollarding is not practiced in the forest now as the industry requires tall straight trees that can be processed mechanically.

Many of the veteran trees in Savernake are out-grown pollards.

Pollarded beech tree

Ancient Oaks

There are as many as a hundred ancient oaks in Savernake and they are some of the oldest living things on Earth. These trees are around 1,000 years old and are in their last stage of life. They are hollow and decaying, yet they still manage to produce new leaves each spring.

The Big Bellied Oak

The most famous of all the trees in Savernake is the Big Bellied Oak, which stands next to the A346 Marlborough to Salisbury road.

Its shape resembles an old-fashioned decanter and because of this it was sometimes known as the Decanter Oak. The name Big Bellied Oak is much more appropriate especially now it has been given a large metal belt to help its big belly from expanding

Duke's Vaunt 1893

further and falling apart!

Hundreds of motorists pass this ancient tree everyday but many don't realise it is one of the oldest surviving trees in the country.

Big Bellied Oak

Duke's Vaunt

The Duke's Vaunt

Another veteran of the forest, not so easily accessible, is the Duke's Vaunt. It can be found deep within the forest, to the east of the Grand Avenue, in Birch Copse. There are no birches here now; instead it is a conifer plantation. Beyond the Crockmere Oak and pool, there is a small gravestone that lies hidden in the undergrowth beside the path. Taking it as your marker, the Duke's Vaunt is a short way into the trees in a north-westerly direction.

This was a truly magnificent tree. Edward Seymour, the Duke of Somerset, was very proud of it and that is how it gained its name. In its prime, it measured 9 metres (30 feet) in circumference on the outside and 6 metres (20 feet) around the inside of its hollow interior. It was so large that at one time a door was added, and as many as twenty boys were able to to be closed inside! On another occasion, a band that included violins, a bassoon and an oboe played within.

A young tree was once planted inside it which grew for some time but eventually died due to the lack of light.

Today, there is only a fraction of the trunk still standing and even that has to be supported. But, despite that, it is worth visiting as

Hollow branch

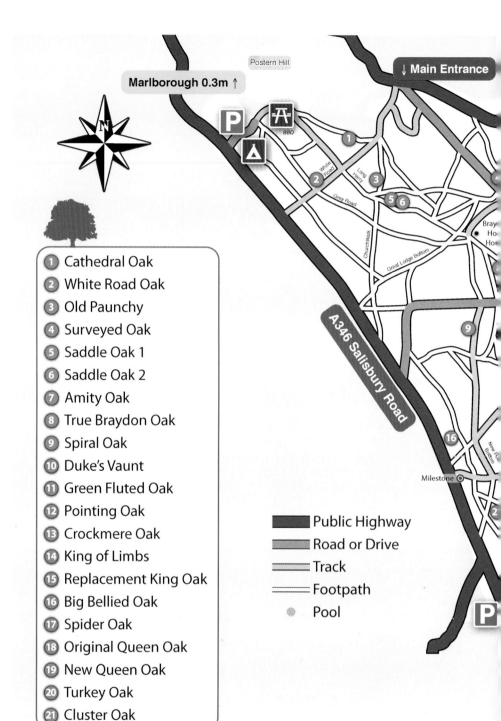

Postern Hill

Marlborough 0.3m ↑

↓ **Main Entrance**

1. Cathedral Oak
2. White Road Oak
3. Old Paunchy
4. Surveyed Oak
5. Saddle Oak 1
6. Saddle Oak 2
7. Amity Oak
8. True Braydon Oak
9. Spiral Oak
10. Duke's Vaunt
11. Green Fluted Oak
12. Pointing Oak
13. Crockmere Oak
14. King of Limbs
15. Replacement King Oak
16. Big Bellied Oak
17. Spider Oak
18. Original Queen Oak
19. New Queen Oak
20. Turkey Oak
21. Cluster Oak

A346 Salisbury Road

Milestone

Public Highway
Road or Drive
Track
Footpath
Pool

Saddle Oak 2

its immenseness can still be visualised. A huge hollow branch lies alongside and acts as a natural water trough for deer and other wildlife. And yet, with only a remnant of the trunk remaining, it still lives and bears one small leafy branch.

King Oak

There is a region along Twelve o'clock Drive that you can find a cluster of ancient oaks. It is here that the King and Queen Oaks are situated. They are named after the two royals famously associated with the area. Unfortunately, the ancient King Oak, that had measured 7 metres (25 feet) in circumference, finally fell only recently but a new strong sapling has been planted as its replacement nearby.

Old Paunchy

Another tree with a big belly! The name is a reference to the rather large protrusion at the bottom of its trunk that resembles a swollen abdomen. This basal swelling occurred after the young tree had been pollarded, which caused it to send up many new shoots from its base. The new growth was repeatedly eaten by animals resulting in a build-up of burr tissue.

Old Paunchy

Twenty boys could fit inside one hollow oak.

Saddle Oaks

Not far from Old Paunchy are two more ancient trees that are a similar shape to each other. Pollarding in their case has caused one branch to grow almost horizontal to the ground.

Many years ago, good-sized branches with bends in them were useful for building large structures such as ships or houses.

Cathedral Oak

The Cathedral Oak's name is a reference to its immense size. Again, it is a tree that was pollarded in earlier times and still has six large limbs emerging from its trunk. Each of these huge branches divides again and again. Even though its gnarled surface is covered in fungi, mosses and ferns, it still looks in good shape. It appears to still be intact although a closer inspection reveals that it too is hollow.

There are many others. Some are named because of their position. For example, the Amity Oak, which lies on the boundary of three parishes; Braydon Oak and the White Road Oak. While others are named after their appearance such as Spiral Oak, Green Fluted Oak and the King of Limbs.

These are just some of the trees that have had their identities labelled, but there are many, many more that remain anonymous.

> Most tree names have evolved from their appearance or their location.

King of Limbs

19

SHAPING THE FOREST

The shape, size and nature of the forest have changed dramatically during its long history. At its greatest extent, it covered 100 square miles, but now it is less than a tenth of the size.

There have been many political and economic changes that have determined how the forest developed.

Before 1066, it was a hunting forest covering approximately 25 square miles. It was an inconvenient arrangement of small patches of woodland scattered beyond the main boundaries, which became difficult to keep under control. So from that time until about 1200, the forest boundary was steadily enlarged to encompass them all.

Areas called 'forest' were not necessarily a continuous wooded area as we understand the term now. It was an area of land scheduled by the King for use as a game reserve. It would have included copses, heaths, woodland and pasture.

The forest was not fenced nor had any visible boundaries and could be very flexible according to the King's whims. Each year, a party of men would ride the outer limits of the forest to establish where the boundaries were.

Savernake became so large that it was divided into five Bailiwicks. The largest of these was La Verme and was the 'home' Bailiwick to the Warden. The others were West Bailiwick, Le Broyle, Hippenscombe and Southgrove. Each one was looked after by a bailiff who was allowed certain privileges, such as pasturing domestic animals; wood for building and maintaining a home; taking fruits from the forest and

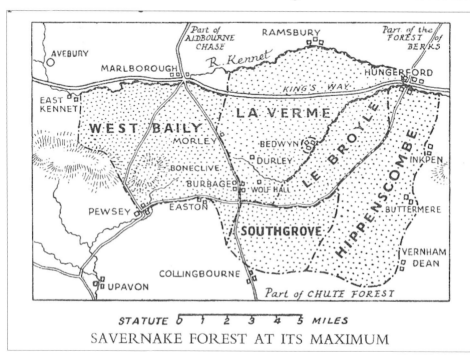

SAVERNAKE FOREST AT ITS MAXIMUM

keeping certain fees and fines inflicted on the resident population.

When Savernake was at its greatest extent, there were eight other forests in Wiltshire: Braydon, Chippenham, Melksham, Selwood, Chute, Clarendon, Melchet and Grovely. There was a danger that if these forests expanded any further they would all have joined together!

It was such a problem that the Magna Carta included two statements concerning the spread of the forests and ordering that forests should be returned to their original size. It was only the beginning of change as a few years later, a supplement known as the Charter of the Forest was signed.

It was an incredibly important document that gave commoners rights and abolished death and mutilation as punishments for forest crimes.

After the reforms, the forests began to drastically reduce in size because they became uneconomic and gradually became established as farmland.

The same fate happened to much of Savernake. The land to the west of the forest as we know it today is now farmland, and the remaining part of the forest is approximately the old Bailiwick of La Verme.

In the second half of the eighteenth century, Lancelot 'Capability' Brown made his mark on Savernake. The way the forest looks today is primarily down

> The term forest did not mean continuous woodland as we know it today.

Ailesbury Column

to him. He envisaged the forest as one great whole and ordered that coppices be joined together by planting hundreds of trees, but not so thickly or uniformly that they looked unnatural. He planned it so that there were openings in the trees so that 'proper objects' could be seen such as Martinsell Hill and various 'follies'.

One of which is the Ailesbury Column that stands on a hill about a mile and a half in front of Tottenham House.

He felt that at every turn there should be some prospect to delight the eye. One of his favourite projects was creating shady rides so that they protected riders from the weather in both the summer and winter.

The Grand Avenue and the crossing point called Eight Walks were created under his direction. It had been planned to erect an octagonal monument at the centre of this unique meeting place but, unfortunately, it was never completed.

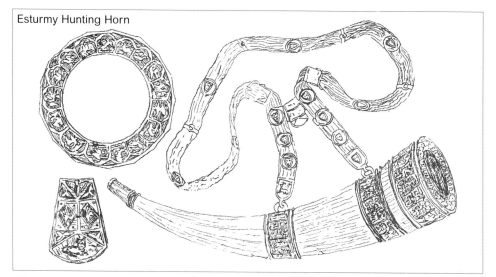

Esturmy Hunting Horn

THE WARDENS

The current Warden of Savernake Forest is the Earl of Cardigan and is the thirty-first to hold the hereditary title.

The Wardenship has been in his family since 1068, when the first Warden, Richard Esturmy, was given the honour by William the Conqueror after fighting with him at the Battle of Hastings.

Savernake was a royal hunting forest and the Warden's role was to protect the game and timber rights for the King.

At that time, he was given official equipment that went with the title. Amongst other things there was a saddle, bridle, sword and a huge ivory silver-edged hunting horn. The horn was always blown to announce the presence of the Sovereign in Savernake and it was a tradition that lasted for many centuries.

These items were badges of office and immediately showed anyone who may not be familiar with him who he was. All of them were handed down to the next in line when the Warden died.

The Warden had certain hereditary rights and privileges and these were confirmed in a charter issued by King John in 1200. Although these rights had existed for 130 years it was the first time they had been put in writing.

On three occasions, there was no male to inherit the title so it passed through the female line resulting in name changes. Firstly, it passed from the Esturmy line to the Seymour's, then to the Bruce line and finally to the Brudenell's who later incorporated the Bruce name to become Brudenell-Bruce.

In the long line of Wardens, there were some that were better at their job than others. Depending on how interested they were in the estate and how their fortunes fared had a lot to do with the forest's development. Because of this, there were some periods of profuse planting and others of neglect.

The Warden's equipment, due to its tremendous age, has long since perished except for the Esturmy hunting horn. It was in the family's possession in Savernake until 1975 when the present Warden's father sold it to the British Museum for £210,000.

FOREST LAW

Since the Medieval period, Royal forests were governed by Forest Law, which was a harsh system that was designed to protect the King's property at the expense of others.

The most serious crimes were killing deer and felling trees. The penalties were brutal and usually meant death or severe mutilation for the offender. Lesser offences such as poaching small game, enclosing land or gathering wood were also judged mercilessly.

However, various licences could be obtained by residents from the Warden to free them from certain restrictions. These, of course, had to be paid for. For example, a Noble could obtain the right to hunt a certain amount of small game annually, or a commoner may ask for the right to gather a quantity of firewood. The Warden was helped in upholding the rules by a team of sub-foresters.

There were Verderers, who looked after the timber; Regarders, who surveyed the land and the Agisters, who oversaw the grazing of animals.

They would meet regularly at the manorial court at Leigh Hill to 'dish out' penalties and fines. More serious crimes were heard by the Justice of the Forest. The court was also the place where licences were granted or renewed and fees were paid. As part of his tenure, the Warden was allowed to keep the fees for certain rights whilst other monies went to the royal exchequer.

As far as the administration was concerned, it meant that a strict eye could be kept on the amount of game and wood that was taken so as not to threaten the quality of the King's hunting, and it also raised a substantial amount of money. In this way, the royal forests' estates became very rich, and this was the reason the boundaries were constantly extended until 1217 when the Charter of the Forest was signed.

JANE SEYMOUR & KING HENRY VIII

Savernake Forest was the birthplace of Jane Seymour, third and favourite wife of King Henry VIII. Jane's father was Sir John Seymour and was the Warden of the forest. He lived at Wolfhall together with his wife and children, and was also a prominent member of Court.

When Jane was old enough, she also went to Court and became a Lady-in-Waiting to Anne Boleyn who was Henry's second wife. Although the King must have been aware that Jane was at Court, it was during a visit to Savernake in 1535 that he began to take a more serious interest in her.

Jane Seymour

King Henry VIII

His queen, Anne, had borne him a daughter but she had failed to produce a son and he was losing patience with her.

At Wolfhall, Jane was required to help her mother with the arrangements and act as hostess during the King's stay.

By the following year, his close attention to Jane did not go unnoticed. She was a complete contrast to Anne with her pale complexion and fair hair.

To make their union possible, Anne was accused of being unfaithful and was sentenced to a public death by decapitation on Tower Hill.

On 20 May 1536, the day after Anne's execution, Henry and Jane were betrothed and were married ten days later.

Henry felt that Jane was his first true wife. He doted on her and she rewarded him with the much-wanted son and heir.

Unfortunately, two weeks after the birth of the prince she died of postnatal complications. Although very weak, she did manage to see her son Edward christened. He was to become King Edward VI.

Henry was heartbroken. He wore black for three months and did not remarry for another three years.

Henry remained on good terms with the Seymour family. Jane's father accompanied the King on several diplomatic trips and was made groom of the bedchamber whilst in France.

Trusted sub-foresters maintained the forest while he was away and everything was still in order when Henry visited again twice more after Jane had died; once in 1539 and again in 1543.

Jane's brother, also named Edward, and the Duke of Somerset, had inevitably risen in importance at Court as the Queen's close relation. He had become the King's personal friend and had proved himself to be trustworthy and very competent.

When the King died in 1547, he was buried beside Jane in a tomb at Windsor Castle; she was the only one of his six wives to be buried there.

Jane Seymour was born and brought up in Savernake.

Prince Edward was only ten years old when his father died so the natural choice of guardian for him was his uncle, Edward Seymour. In this role, Jane's brother became Governor of the King and Lord Protector of The Realm. He also had become the Warden of Savernake when his father died.

In 1548, Edward Seymour finally became the absolute owner of Savernake by royal grant. It was the first time that ownership of an entire forest had been given to a subject, and it is still the only forest in private ownership to this day.

On behalf of the prince, he ruled England for three years until jealous rivals were successful in plotting against him. He was imprisoned in the Tower of London and tried for treason and felony. He was executed in 1552.

Edward Seymour

Wolfhall Barn

Ancient Barn at Wolfhall - Scene of Marriage Feast of Henry VIII & Lady Jane Seymour
A Sketch after that by Revd George Stallard in Wiltshire Archaeological Magazine
Only the left hand portion now remains

WOLFHALL

Unfortunately, the extensive timber-framed mansion that was Wolfhall no longer exists, but its part in the forest's history is an important one. It was the home of the young Jane Seymour, who became King Henry VIII's third wife, Queen of England and mother of King Edward VI.

The name had nothing to do with wolves. They incidentally had become extinct in Savernake by the end of the fifteenth century. Instead, it was derived from the Danish or Saxon name Ulph, and

Henry VIII stayed
at Wolfhall
on three occasions.

Wolfhall was the home
of the Warden of
Savernake.

the house is referred to as Ulfela in the Domesday Book.

There are still clues to its existence. On the road from Crofton to Burbage is a farm called Wolfhall Farm. The current farmhouse, known as Wolfhall Manor, was built later than the original Wolfhall.

The earlier house had been laid out in a rectangular pattern with two internal courts and a chapel. It was surrounded by gardens designed for pleasure with names such as 'Myn Old Lady's Gardyne' and 'Myn Young Lady's Gardyne'. The house must have been almost self-sufficient as it had its own brewery, kitchen gardens and an orchard.

The household employed as many as 50 servants in various occupations. Nearby, there still is a house known as The Laundry, which is thought to be a reference to the old house. It can be identified by its impressive chimneys.

Wolfhall, although comfortable, was not grand nor built for lavish entertaining. So when the King came to visit Sir John to go hunting in the forest, it required a huge amount of organisation to accommodate him and his entourage.

The old barn was transformed into a banqueting hall after a thorough clean and hung with tapestries.

The King and his closest courtiers would have stayed in the main house while less important members of the Seymour family withdrew to the hunting lodge, and other guests would have stayed at neighbouring houses overnight. The King liked it so much he stayed there on three occasions.

According to local folklore, the royal wedding was supposed to have taken place in the barn at Wolfhall, but this, in all probability, is unlikely.

The house's demise came about within the next generation of Seymours. After Sir Edward became Lord Protector of the Realm, he was required to be in London most of the time. And after his premature death, his heir was a prisoner in the Tower. There was no one to maintain the old building and it was left to decay.

Interestingly, a remnant of the old Wolfhall still exists and can be seen in the church at Great Bedwyn. There you can find a stained glass window that was saved from the ruins. Made between 1537 and 1546 when Edward VI was Prince of Wales, it features the Imperial Crown, the badge of Jane Seymour, the Prince of Wales Feathers and a Tudor Rose.

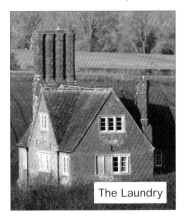
The Laundry

Wolfhall's window

27

TOTTENHAM HOUSE

Tottenham House is situated on the south-eastern edge of the forest near the end of the Grand Avenue. It is a splendid example of a Palladian-style mansion with beautiful proportions and curved wings on either side of the main building.

The house started as the forest's hunting lodge. When Wolfhall was no longer inhabitable, the sixteenth Warden, the Earl of Hertford, chose to move his residence to the lodge which was only about a mile away. He began to improve and extend the old lodge by recycling building materials from the crumbling Wolfhall. This was in 1575 and it was just the beginning of many more attempts at enhancement.

The next major remodelling was 160 years later when the twenty-first Warden, the Earl of Ailesbury, asked his brother-in-law, the architect Lord Burlington, to build a house in the fashionable Palladian style. This Warden employed 'Capability' Brown to improve the forest which included the planting of the Grand Avenue.

Bruce's nephew, the twenty-third Warden, was created Marquess of Ailesbury, a position that elevated him above his neighbours. In his opinion, the old house built by Lord Burlington was not grand enough for his new status.

So, in 1820, he enlisted a new architect, Thomas Cundy, who cleverly surrounded the old house entirely, incorporating it into the new design. The old brickwork was completely covered with gleaming Bath stone.

It was built for entertaining on a grand scale having a series of large reception rooms that opened into one another. These

Tottenham House

Tottenham House 1740

were sumptuously decorated with marble which was laid by Italian craftsmen.

Overall, there were more than 100 rooms and each of these was filled with the latest Empire-style furniture from Paris. All the old Queen Anne furniture of his uncle's was deemed too old-fashioned and was thrown out!

The cost even at that time was huge, totalling more than £250,000.

The cream of society was entertained in style. The Prince of Wales is known to have stayed at the house on several occasions.

Unfortunately, later generations found it too costly to maintain. In its heyday, to maintain the standards in the house and grounds a hundred staff were employed. Even without entertaining, it was impossible to run the house efficiently on any less than twenty four.

The financial burden was such a strain that after the Second World War the family moved to a smaller house in the forest.

Tottenham House was leased to a boys' school and subsequently to the Amber Foundation which was a charity for unemployed young people.

Still the costs of maintaining the building were impossibly high and it gradually fell into disrepair. Some parts of the house became semi-derelict and English Heritage placed it on their 'at risk' register as it is a Grade I listed building.

Recently, a lease was negotiated with a company planning to convert the house and some of the grounds into a luxury hotel and golf course. A £135 million budget was set for the project, an equivalent sum to the amount paid by the Marquess for the remodelling in 1820.

> A hundred staff were employed to run the house.

Remains of ammunition shelter

WARTIME SAVERNAKE

Savernake's location was ideal for it to be used as an ammunition store during World War II. It was far enough away from London not to threaten the safety of such a large population yet it had good road and rail access from the Capital. It was also close to the army training ground of Salisbury Plain, and not too far from the south coast allowing an easy route for ammunition to cross the Channel.

The trees made excellent cover both on the ground and from aircraft flying overhead. In the event of an explosion, either accidental or from enemy attack, the greater part of the impact would be absorbed by the trees.

Soon after war was declared,

the British Army moved in and set up camps in the forest. Tottenham House was requisitioned and used for administration and also as accommodation for some of the higher ranking officers. The Warden and his family were moved into the attic apartments to make room for them.

Later, from 1942 until 1945, the forest was under the command of the American Forces and this was when it was at its most active. There were as many as 350 American and 200 British personnel on the site.

After the War had ended and up to 1949, it was back under

After the war the Forestry Commission used some of the huts to store acorns.

British control and was used to store ammunition brought back from the continent.

In the forest today, you can see many rectangular areas that have been dug out along the main avenue and other side roads. These are what remain of the shelters used to store the shells and chemical material.

The one pictured is the remains of a Nissen type shelter. It had end walls made of brick with a concrete floor that was divided into twelve bays. The roof was corrugated steel and the whole thing would have been covered in earth to act as a buffer in case of accidents.

In one such incident in July 1945, an ammunition store caught fire and exploded. It caused a huge amount of damage to property and resulted in the loss of life of an American serviceman.

Then, only six months later, there was another enormous explosion. This time in one of 100 wagons that was carrying munitions back from Europe. It was thought to have been caused by a German booby-trapped mine; it set off a succession of detonations throughout the wagons. The force was so great that windows as far away as Marlborough and St Katharine's Church were blown out.

If it was not for the bravery of the men who moved the wagons away from the danger zone, it could have been a lot worse. As it was, eight men died and many more were injured.

The George Cross was issued to two of the soldiers in recognition of their heroism and courage in the extreme danger. The medal is the highest gallantry award for civilians and military personnel in non-combat situations.

All 400 deer were shot except 12 red and 12 fallow when the deer park was ploughed in 1941.

Rear view of Tottenham House

TIMELINE

	Primeval Forest
	Ancient oaks established
1066	Norman Conquest
1200	King John's Charter confirms hereditary rights of the Wardens
1427	Hereditary Warden title passed from the Esturmy to the Seymour line
1535	King Henry VIII: a guest at Wolfhall
1536	King Henry VIII marries Jane Seymour
1537	Edward VI born
1539 & 1543	King Henry VIII: a guest at Wolfhall
1547	King Henry VIII died
1548	Savernake becomes private property by royal grant
1575	Wardens moved to Tottenham Lodge from Wolfhall
1676	Hereditary Warden title passed from Seymour to Bruce line
1735	Tottenham House remodelled by Lord Burlington
1740	Grand Avenue planted
1747	Hereditary Warden title passed to Brudenell-Bruce line
1820	Present Tottenham House built
1939	Forest leased to Forestry Commission
1940-9	Forest used by military as ammunitions store
1975	Esturmy Hunting Horn sold to British Museum
201?	Tottenham House to become luxury hotel